Sarah Ferguson is an award-winning investi-
gative journalist at the ABC. She wrote *The
Killing Season Uncut* with Patricia Drum in
2016.

Writers in the *On Series*

Fleur Anderson

Gay Bilson

John Birmingham

Julian Burnside

Blanche d'Alpuget

Paul Daley

Robert Dessaix

Juliana Engberg

Sarah Ferguson

Nikki Gemmell

Stan Grant

Germaine Greer

Sarah Hanson-Young

Jonathan Holmes

Daisy Jeffrey

Susan Johnson

Malcolm Knox

Barrie Kosky

Sally McManus

David Malouf

Paula Matthewson

Katharine Murphy

Dorothy Porter

Leigh Sales

Mark Scott

Tory Shepherd

Tim Soutphommasane

David Speers

Natasha Stott Despoja

Anne Summers

Tony Wheeler

Ashleigh Wilson

Elisabeth Wynhausen

Sarah Ferguson
On
Mother

hachette
AUSTRALIA

Every attempt has been made to locate the copyright holders for
material quoted in this book. Any person or organisation that may
have been overlooked or misattributed may contact the publisher.

Published in Australia and New Zealand in 2020
by Hachette Australia
(an imprint of Hachette Australia Pty Limited)
Level 17, 207 Kent Street, Sydney NSW 2000
www.hachette.com.au

First published in 2018 by Melbourne University Publishing

10 9 8 7 6 5 4 3 2 1

A catalogue record for this
book is available from the
National Library of Australia

ISBN: 978 0 7336 4416 0 (paperback)

Original cover concept by Nada Backovic Design
Text design by Alice Graphics
Typeset by Typeskill
Printed and bound in Australia by McPherson's Printing Group

MIX
Paper from
responsible sources
FSC® C001695

The paper this book is printed on is certified against the
Forest Stewardship Council® Standards. McPherson's Printing
Group holds FSC® chain of custody certification SA-COC-005379.
FSC® promotes environmentally responsible, socially beneficial

To Anthony

I talked to my mother throughout the summer, floating in the ocean, head tilted back in the water, eyes skyward. On days when the swell was too strong, I drifted in the tea-tree-stained water of the creek. There where no one could hear, I spoke out loud the words and names not used since childhood. I thanked her, as I had for the first time weeks earlier, reaching forward tentatively to stroke her soft grey hair on the pillow. I talked to her in the garden where I made my first flowerbed, for her; English flowers, hollyhocks and grandmother's bonnets, deep purple lavender. I told her how like the bed beyond her kitchen window it was. *I who have never grown anything anywhere, have made a whole bed grow riotously for you in the hard Australian sun.* She smiled and made a face as if to say, *That's a turn-up for the books, you in the garden with secateurs and twine. Now I've heard it all.*

I talked to her during the summer sport, the Ashes and the Open, because Marjorie was a true aficionado, with a near obsession for the Swiss tennis player. She had a similar obsession with Pakistani cricketer Imran Khan, to the point where my father would hide copies of books about him under the bed. We spent a lot of time in my childhood, she and I, watching cricket. It never seemed odd, though I realise now it might seem so. We talked seriously about the game, but the subject of those afternoons was really love, a mother's love, imparted wordlessly at a provincial cricket ground with scorecards, a thermos and tartan rugs against the English summer cold. You might say it was an English form of love, oblique, unable to be stated, but it wasn't. I don't think my generation, which expresses love so easily and so often, loves any more or provides more security by declaring it in every phone call. I knew her love was there, I knew it with complete and easy certainty, as it was in countless other scenes in the landscapes we shared.

'I have lived so far away for so long, I'm sorry,' I tried to say. But she wouldn't allow it. She never said don't move so far, or it would make me happy if you came home, or even that it was hard for her. She understood and she didn't know reproach. She had left her own parents in Nairobi in 1959, aged twenty-three, her mother at the open door, fierce with recrimination, imploring her daughter not to leave. She took a taxi from the house, through the game park to the airport, and boarded a plane for the long journey to England. A polite, obedient young woman who had come of age in the middle-class world of postwar England was marrying against her parents' wishes. She lived her own life and encouraged me to do the same. She would not accept the sorrow, even as the words formed on my lips.

'Hush,' she said. 'You have nothing to be sorry for.'

❧

In early September, my husband, Tony, and I boarded a plane in Melbourne. A WhatsApp message flashed on my phone. *Can you ring me immediately. Ta.* An odd mix of urgent and casual, it was from my brother, Anthony, in London, where it was the middle of the night. I felt a bolt of fear and smothered it. I decided to wait till I landed. We left Sydney airport in a taxi, and as we turned the corner away from the terminal, the last thing I noticed were the billboards and a doughnut store up ahead. I called his number.

'What's up?'

'I don't know how to say it so I'll just say it. Mother died.'

The bonds broke, snapping and uncoiling, like a thousand tiny ropes. I cried out. Tony tried to hold me, but I couldn't be held. Decades of restraint unravelled. The driver heard my cries and faced forward, head slightly bowed.

No.

On a broken line, Anthony tried to explain. 'She was alone in hospital. We didn't know she was there.'

No, no, not by herself, I sobbed. *It's so wrong.*

Anthony wasn't in London. He was in Italy, driving through the tunnels in the Alps towards Milan airport. The signal dropped out.

Not by herself. Not alone. No. I thrashed about in the back of the taxi, like something animal.

The phone rang again.

I urged myself to think of him, in the dark, racing for a flight.

'I'm sorry you had to make this call.'

'I don't know much,' he said. His children were on their way to the hospital.

I learned the children's story later. Hospital staff had rung the house but much too late. My niece and nephew struggled to find their way there in the dark; so impoverished are English councils that they switch off the streetlights at night, which made it nearly impossible for the children to find their way. They don't do that in the tiny NSW hamlet where I live, population 242, where a bright light illuminates the few streets through the night, competing with the Milky Way. They incurred a fine for driving in a bus lane that had no buses at night, then in the dimly lit hospital car park, they poured money into an expensive ticket machine, thinking they would be there for hours. Inside, a junior doctor showed them to their grandmother, who had died minutes earlier. Not knowing what to do next, they went to her house and sat in her sitting room, every creak and groan of wind and wood jolting them to fear, waiting for dawn and another drive, to Heathrow to collect their parents. My mother, their grandmother, lay in the hospital, alone, dead, having spoken her last words to a harried nurse, 'I'm clammy and cold.'

As a reporter, my working life is immersed in loss. People damaged by violence and hatred, epochal suffering from wars or natural disaster, the unforgettable hardship of children, human baseness in all its forms. It leaves lines in your soul and fills me with respect for the sufferer. In Aceh, 170,000 people died in the Boxing Day tsunami. The surviving adults were anguished for the souls of the unburied dead, whose cries they heard coming from the riverbeds at night, especially those of the dead children. They implored the former President Wahid, a spiritual man, to come to Aceh and say prayers that would allow the dead to rest. More recently, in a village in Lebanon close to the Syrian border, I met a man called Hussain whose eight children had drowned in a smuggler's rotten boat, only a short distance from the Javanese shore they had left en route to Australia. It was his idea for the family to make the journey and only he survived. As the boat broke up, the children were thrown into the ocean, the youngest slipping from his grasp. All eight of them washed up lifeless on the shore. Squatting on his heels below a crumbling minaret, he watched as villagers measured out and dug squat graves, in preparation for the return of the children's bodies from Indonesia, sent by plane in rough coffins, kept cold on the journey to Beirut. Closer to home are the mothers and fathers, brothers and sisters of murdered or damaged children whose names I keep to myself. Who am I to write about loss when mine is so small, so ordinary?

I have come to understand that the comparison has no meaning and to stop apologising for my sadness. A mother's love is so exquisite as to be beyond comparison; it is not measured on a scale. I lost something true, not perfect, even odd at times, but the surest thing on earth that I have known.

❦

Tony and I caught a flight to London a few hours after Anthony's call. It was the second time I had flown back to the United Kingdom summoned by family loss. On that first occasion, it was for my father's death. This time I had Tony with me, tenderly clearing a path so I wouldn't encounter anything harsh or careless. Moving through the busy airport, the sounds seemed muted, as if coming from far away. Another driver, told of the reason for the journey, offered his condolences with halting delicacy. We left the suburbs of London, asphalt giving way to the green of East Anglia's farming country. From the dull dread deep in my stomach, panic rose upwards. *Don't take the next turn-off. Stay on the road. Drive past it, don't turn left. Ignore the GPS. Don't drive in there. Don't stop the car, or get out, don't unload the suitcases. Don't bring me here. To her house. I hardly know where to begin.*

I pulled the heavy doorbell. My mother should have come to the door, brisk, 'there you are', as if it were a daily event, disguising the excitement or allowing herself to parcel it out, not use it all up in a noisy, clamorous moment, as I would. She was more discreet, less voluble. I want to write that she was gentler than I am, better, but she won't let me. Instead of her, my brother, Anthony, stood in the hall. Our usual language was humour, teasing each other in ways that shocked others. Growing up, I was both his younger sister and his frontman, doing the hard jobs, collecting wayward balls from scary neighbours, confessing we had stolen walnuts from Mrs Wall's tree. There was too much to say to begin, so for now we just embraced.

The house was full. Emily Dickinson says there is nothing so solemn as the bustle in a house after death. There were neighbours, a minister, my brother's children, his kind wife, Sarah, pouring tea from the big silver teapot with the wooden handle. A flash of memory came from a photo: the patio of their Lagos home, Goriola Street, my mother sitting in a pink Nigerian dress embroidered with white, her legs tucked elegantly to the side, a baby in her lap, and behind her, tea laid out. It was 1964. The teapot survived all the tumult that followed: the outbreak of war, the move to Scotland. The dress, I wore to pieces after my mother gave it to me.

I stood still just inside the kitchen door, noticing things around me. The wrong things, a pair of leather slippers beneath a stool, the calendar with today's date and an appointment, two newspapers in their plastic wrap. The minister brushed the white flecks from his trousers, then shifted in his chair. *These aren't her guests, why are we here without her?* It took moments for the visitors to sense the shock I had brought with me into the room. The kindly neighbours from the other side of the hawthorn hedge, both tall, bent down towards me to offer their sympathies.

'Thank you for your great kindness to her,'
I said. I meant it, but I didn't mean to speak
of her as gone. The house was still holding
her here in a spell.

Only then I noticed my uncle, her twin
brother, John, sitting in the corner, shrunken
and uncertain. I had rung him hours earlier
from Sydney airport, walking through the
brassy terminal. For the only time in my life,
he told me how he felt. 'I'm distraught,' he
said. It is one of the saddest things I have ever
heard. As children in Harrogate at different
schools, each twin knew when the other was
in pain or distress. In the earliest photograph
I have of my mother and uncle, they are four
years old, dressed in matching coats with
double buttons and Peter Pan collars. Mother
wears a hat with a fringe poking through,

and they are clutching toy African animals, I guess to keep them still for the photographer. Marjorie is not focusing on the camera, she is looking the right way, but her gaze is tentative. It is the same in almost every photo, always looking somewhere beyond the lens, shy perhaps, but also withholding something.

The day she left her parents' home in Nairobi, she sent a telegram to her twin on the other side of the world, telling him she was leaving to marry Iain in Scotland on Boxing Day. John had just returned to the United Kingdom from flight training in Canada and didn't receive the telegram. Marjorie knew she would be alone for the wedding, but she wanted him to know. She made the journey alone from Nairobi via Entebbe, Khartoum, Libya and Rome. Once in Scotland, she gave herself over to her future husband's relatives, not all welcoming; a sort of elopement from Africa for the prodigal son was too much for some of them. One aunt offered the general view, in the broad accent of Fife, 'At least she's no' black.'

On the morning of the wedding on 26 December 1959, sure of her decision, forthright but alone nonetheless, Marjorie answered a knock at the front door of her sister-in-law's house. John was standing on the doorstep, snow on the shoulders of his heavy dark overcoat. 'Hello, Twin,' he said, grinning.

It wasn't until I was about to get married that my childish lack of curiosity gave way. Wanting to know the real story is the single most important driver of my profession, but for years their wedding photos had not prompted me to ask why Uncle John was by my mother's side instead of my grandfather, why the wedding was in Scotland rather than at her home in Lagos, and why they had married on Boxing Day?

⁂

I thought Uncle John's anguished cry that I had heard on the phone from thousands of kilometres away meant we would talk now about what had happened to my mother. I was wrong.

'Come on, lass, we need a walk,' he said.

We went into the fields, late-summer blackberries heavy on the hedgerows, wood pigeons rising suddenly with great clatter, but he would not talk about her. He told me that my questions about what had caused her death had no purpose. 'The answers won't change anything.' He reverted to the safe subjects, British and European politics. There is no place for judgement in shock. I crossed the stile back towards the house, holding my questions in.

❧

The first thing I learned after we landed in London was that there was no funeral to plan. My mother's body was being held in the hospital morgue because the cause of death was unexplained. The first question was, would we see the body there? Despite the mayhem of my career, those closest to me know I am squeamish, no good with blood, but there is something more. I fear the terrible image that would be held in vivid perpetuity in my mind's eye. I don't avoid the grim details of a story, but I have often protected myself from images that my eye and soul won't bear. Uncle John had already said he didn't want to see her in the morgue. My dearest, oldest friend, Lucy, who by chance was staying nearby, warned me not to do it. I knew I had to go. I feared the ordinary as much as the gruesome, or some whiff of functionality. It was a morgue, after all.

Years earlier my father had died so well, his final days spent over a fortnight at home surrounded by his family. Anthony and I slept in single beds in a spare room, like children again. My mother, made uncertain by distress, took to sitting at her dressing table looking out at the fields, talking gently to my father as he lay barely conscious in the bed behind. That was my idea. An older member of the family had tried to push my mother out of the way, to be closer to his death bed, the death catcher, the significant one. I saw what was happening and told my mother that she didn't need to hold his hand every moment and count his breaths, just sit nearby with her jewellery boxes and creams, her dressing-table things, in silence if she wanted. Before he became unconscious, my father lost some inhibitions. His mellow Scottish accent broadened, he took to sending visitors away, shouting from upstairs to the hallway below. My favourite was a phrase I had never heard before, to an unwanted churchman. As he turned to leave, my father bellowed, 'I hope your tennis racket splits in the middle!' That was telling him.

In the end, it was Anthony and I who were with him when he took his final breath. The breaths had become long and ragged, and we had got used to waiting. We waited again, looked at each other, giggled for a moment in the tension, then understood. Afterwards we looked after him with tenderness, ringing Anthony's Irish mother-in-law, Tras, for advice. The Irish do this better than the English. Did we even put coins on his eyes to pay the ferry man as if it were the nineteenth century, or did I imagine that? We drank whisky together, clinking our glasses over his body. A huge storm whipped around the house, lifting the roof off, or so it seemed. It was a Rabbie Burns night, ripe for a Scot; my mother said the storm had carried him away. She didn't mean it, but the image was right. From then I wanted to do everything—carry the body down the stairs, not hitting the bannister as I heard the undertakers do, drive the hearse, dig a grave or scatter the ashes—everything done perfectly without a false move or note.

For my mother, it was different in every way. She had been alone. People who did not know her were with her as she neared death, then died. I read their six-word description in the hospital investigation. 'Pupils dilated. Pt has passed away.'

No one held her hand or kissed her forehead, told her it was time to go. It wasn't time nor was it gentle. It was rough and mechanical and she was alone. And as they must, they moved her away and carried on with the living.

Now she was in a morgue. Watched over by God knows whom.

The four of us went together. I am Sarah, my husband is Anthony (Tony). My brother is Anthony, his wife is Sarah. The Anthonys and Sarahs went in the car together to the morgue.

❧

A skinny man in a beige tunic was waiting for us at the front door of the morgue, a small, low-rise 1950s administrative block with a big round window of frosted glass. Who would want to look through this round window, I wondered? I tried to ignore the questions provoked by the tall chimney that rose behind the building. The man told us his name was H, which was odd, but there was no place here for inquiries.

'Spend as much time as you want in there.' He pointed across the hallway. 'I'll be in the office.'

Now it was happening, worse than the car, worse than the house. Is haywire a word? I felt my brain was going haywire. Anthony and I went first. He opened the door to a simple room with a single bed, like a platform, draped in white, a secular room with a few notes borrowed from religion. On the bed was a body beneath the shroud, a thin covering for the mechanics of death, the white sheet brought up close to the chin. Anthony told me afterwards he thought it wasn't her, that they had the wrong person. I saw the tears in his eyes.

My response was to run out. I couldn't be in here.

I went back in with Tony, staying at the end of the bed, relatively safe. I went in and out a few times until I was able to stay alone. How unlike the living self is our dead self. I still wasn't sure I was looking at my mother. I edged towards the head on the pillow. Then all of a sudden it was her. Somewhere in the profile, the shape of the large nose, beyond the bruising and the absence, the stone still-ness, she was there. I began to form words.

'Mummy. It's alright, sweetheart. It's alright. Thank you, sweetheart.' I'd never spoken to her like that before. I should have, part child, part adult, childlike and motherly. I repeated the words I had found.

'Thank you, sweetheart. It's alright now.'

I reached forward to stroke her hair, it was so soft, then I misjudged the movement and touched the skin, so cold and unyielding. Death was here. I recoiled, paused then leaned forward again, spoke the same words and stroked her hair again. 'Thank you for everything,' I said as tears rolled down my face. I could have lain down next to her. If she had been at home I may have, but not in this strange resting place. I wanted her to live forever, but she didn't.

❧

Anthony and I sat on the sofa in my mother's sitting room with a box of slides and black-and-white photos on our knees, passing the pictures back and forth. There were so few things in the house we could touch. It was her house, quiet and still and full of her in every part of it. The slides were from Nigeria in the 1960s. An attractive young mother in pale blue shorts and a white bikini top, with a child dressed as Batman playing at her feet. In every shot she had poise—lady-like would be the description of the time. So unlike me, I thought; a friend once told me I walked like a boxer. Another photo taken at Tarkwa Bay showed her laughing in the surf, holding a child, with the strap of her bathing costume slipped down. I held the small white Kodachrome squares up to the light; we hadn't looked at these pictures for years. A few of the shots were professional photographs at events where she wore elegant dresses made from Yoruba fabrics, dancing with my father, who was an excellent dancer, in a smooth 1950s way. Her gaze was always somewhere beyond the camera.

Marjorie would have called herself shy, but she was also bold. When she was pregnant for the first time, the local doctor advised her to go see 'Dr DC10' and made a motion with his hand into the air. She waited for him to explain. 'Take the DC10 to London, have your baby there, madam.' That's what white women did. She refused. If the Nigerian women had their babies in Lagos, why wouldn't she? My father's employer sent a deputation to the house to tell him that my mother should change her mind. London was the right place for women to be. We were born in Lagos. There was never any fuss surrounding these decisions, but my mother could not be persuaded. I was born on New

Year's Eve. I recalled her description of the smiling Nigerian gynaecologist appearing at the hospital in a dinner jacket and black tie.

There were a few mementos of Africa in her house, a painting of the Rift Valley, a little fragile ivory lion and its cub, a silver cigarette box from a Lagos golf club. I remember as a child how much I loved the unfamiliar word engraved on the lid, 'Ikoyi', and its hint of places far away. Marjorie loved Africa, but when they moved back to the United Kingdom she began again, she didn't dwell. I think she thought it was disloyal to the present to live in the past. She was quiet and bold, conservative and flexible and loyal.

There was a rare shot in the photo box of her looking straight at the camera, taken before she got married, in the garden of her parents' home in Nairobi in 1959. She wore capri pants, ballet shoes and a white tunic. She was sitting on a low wall, her hands clasped around her shins. My father had written 'My darling' on the back with a question mark. Early days.

In the 1950s, my grandparents went to Kenya for my grandfather to run the East African bus company. He did not encourage his daughters, Marjorie and Helen, to join them. Nairobi had a reputation as a fast town. Marjorie insisted they go anyway. The girls earned their own money to pay for one-way tickets on the Union-Castle line and headed to Mombasa.

She made these decisions and I admired her for it. It was harder to resist your parents' wishes then. But it was the same characteristic that meant she refused to tell us she was going to hospital in an ambulance after a fall at home. Why didn't she tell us, call me and say she was fine, how stupid and boring it was and that she had tickets to the next tennis tournament in London and she would be going?

I walked around the empty rooms in the house, looking for her in the absence. In the bedroom, the latest copy of *The Spectator* was under her pillow. She thought she was coming back. I sat at her dressing table. On the window ledge were binoculars that she would seize up when she spied a bird in the meadow. I saw the rose she had trained to run along the rear fence, a bright red punctuation before the fields beyond.

We had made the kitchen more normal by our presence, but the atoms in the sitting room seemed barely to have moved. I ran my fingers along the polished walnut of the folded bridge table. In the far corner on a side table were her recent books, two neat piles of biographies and histories—Gainsborough, the Romanovs, Churchill—all non-fiction, like the bookshelves where Obama and Robert E Lee sat next to each other. There were only a few novels in the house.

Marjorie admired intelligence and felt she lacked something for not having gone to university. She took courses—English painters, the American revolution—her essays filed in neat exercise books. I sat at her little desk. There was a yellow legal pad, with lines of her handwriting. I could hardly bear to look at it, so near to her soul. The pity of it. I made out the writing, not as strong as it had been, 'Our friendship goes back many years. Inge always calls me "darling", which I really love.' What made her write it? Practising for a birthday card, perhaps.

Why can't I talk to you when I can hear you in those words? I tugged at the drawers, uncertain what I was looking for. In the top drawer were copies of recent letters, one to the horticultural society questioning their judging protocols, another to the chairman of the Tory Party, remonstrating against the conduct of the Brexit referendum.

> *I voted to remain in the EU and very little has gone right since that fateful decision. I don't know what a 'hard Brexit' means and I imagine there are plenty like me, so someone must start explaining what lies ahead …*

She signed off,

You and your colleagues have let us down
very badly.
Yours sincerely,
Marjorie Ferguson

She and John had fallen out over Brexit. She had loved politics all her life and expected us to follow the national debate. After the move from Nigeria, canvassing in the streets of Aberdeen, aged five, I would march along beside her. She taught me the campaign song for one of the most unorthodox MPs ever to stand for parliament, Mad Colin Mitchell. A portion of the tune came back.

Vote vote vote for Colin Mitchell
You can't vote for a better man

Dum di dum di dum
And we'll have him if we can
And we'll throw Laura Grimond in the Dee.

Laura Grimond was a Liberal with a distinguished heritage, granddaughter of Prime Minister Herbert Asquith and not at all deserving of the icy waters of the Dee. Marjorie was a partisan Tory, but in later years she took to reading the left-wing *New Statesman* as well as *The Spectator* because she said the writing was better.

I looked out of the window to the fields. An early-autumn sun picked out the last meadow flowers, and in the distance the spire of the village church showed just above the tree line, a rare high point in the flat countryside. Marjorie's gardens, her humour, her

steadfastness, it suggested something quin-
tessentially English, a respect for tradition,
but in her case without fetishising it, capable
of change.

Marjorie and my father did not return
to Kenya after they married. Instead, they
moved to Nigeria. It was unclear to me
whether they had been welcome back in
Nairobi. What was it that had put my grandparents so firmly against the marriage?
Before she arrived, it was they who had asked
the handsome Scot to show Marjorie around
Nairobi. He was a bachelor living in the
Gaylord Hotel, with a Riley Pathfinder to get
around town. He drove in the East African
rally and taught Marjorie to drive on the quiet
roads of the game park. She always loved fast
cars. The closest I got to an explanation for

my grandparents' objection to the marriage was that by then my father was between jobs, but that didn't seem to justify the intensity of my grandmother's opposition. A relative once whispered that he may have punched someone, but the subject was long closed. After the move to Nigeria, Marjorie didn't see her parents for ten years, not until my father brokered a peace one year when they were on leave. She remembered them stopping in a layby to gather themselves before driving to the house in Suffolk. The tension evaporated from then, she said. It was not visible to me as a child, but then I didn't look.

They lived on Victoria Island near the Bight of Benin, picnicking under palm trees at Tarkwa Bay, frequenting a nightclub called the Bagatelle. The country was emerging from colonial rule, and many of their friends in the photos were from the new generation of well-educated Nigerians. My mother remembered the history well, telling the story of the first prime minister who was murdered, Abubaker Tafawa Balewa, the name rolling off her tongue as if everyone knew it. When the Biafran War broke out, my parents had to quit Nigeria but not in a hurry. As the Biafran forces reached within 130 miles of Lagos, the expat community was gripped by panic. Marjorie refused to be evacuated with the American wives to ships waiting in the gulf, instead she went to town to get her hair done.

I found a slim paperback on the shelves in the sitting room, *Hausa for Beginners*. How had that survived? Hausa is the language of the Muslim north of the country, where they travelled together, my father carrying large sums of cash for tribal leaders, or emirs.

I leaned against the shelves reading the chapter titled 'Breakdown'.

'*Allah ya sa*. God has caused. A Hausa speaks of God where we often speak of luck or chance. *Tana rawa* means dance, shake or tremble. *Rawa daji* means prancing-about-in-the bush.'

God has caused. Why had I never asked my mother about the dislocation of moving from Nigeria to Aberdeen? She had a cook in Nigeria who could make beef Wellington for twelve. I don't know why I remember that. Who would want to eat beef Wellington in Lagos?

My mother never said the move to Scotland was hard, but it must have been.

Exchanging the great ball of the African sun for the grey granite of Aberdeen and the cold. The city is so far north that in winter there are only six hours of daylight. She always loved the sun, turned her face towards it, closing her eyes. When we were old enough to go to primary school, Anthony said the obvious thing: she was always there, not exactly like other mothers, eccentric even, but there at every moment of our childhood, near and kind. So different to my life. My children could say I was hardly ever there, frequently travelling, not often at the school gate. She never criticised me, no more than the occasional exclamation of 'Sarah!' coming across the pockets of chaos in our lives. She was funny. When we watched the cricket, Anthony and his friends sat behind running a comic commentary. She pretended not to listen, eyes focused on the pitch, but she giggled along with them. When as an adult Anthony ran an annual cricket game in the village, he chose her as the umpire. She couldn't tell a joke herself, always starting in the middle then starting again. And she was a stickler for the facts. She wouldn't allow my father, the natural storyteller, his exaggerations, one lion not three, Kano not Kenya. Now there is no one left to check my story.

❦

Our youngest son, Lucien, had arrived from Madrid, Cosmo was on his way from Australia. Like my niece and nephew, Lucien brought life with him. We went to a local pub for lunch. This was Essex where the accents swing between horse and hounds and footballers made good. I wanted to tell them that this was my pub, that I had lived there and drunk at the bar long before they got there, before it was primped and turned into a gastro pub. It was just warm enough to sit outside. Anthony, Tony and Lucien cleared the chestnut pods and leaves from the outdoor pool table. It was good to be together, and we laughed for the first time. I even took a few photos.

Anthony's phone rang. He moved away from the table, standing very straight, the phone to his ear. 'Right. I see.'

It was the coroner's office. The day stopped. The brief moment of goodness was extinguished. The cause of her death could not be explained, so there would be an inquest.

The others abandoned the game, leaning the pool cues against the table. Instead of going home, we drove through narrow lanes to the village church, the trees bending over on either side of it, barely leaving room for the car. Tony and I were married here, Anthony and I used to come on Christmas Eve with our parents, not out of faith but faithful to a village life lived over 900 years since the church was built. In the bleak midwinter long, long ago. We opened the gate and walked through the ancient churchyard subdued.

❧

I can hear echoes of Philip Larkin throughout this story. I wrote to Larkin as a teenager on decorated notepaper, questioning his bleak view on life. He replied from his post at Hull University, pointing me towards a line in 'Dockery and Son', 'Life is first boredom then fear.' This view was unintelligible to me, but 'Church Going' and other poems I understood.

> Since someone will forever be surprising
> A hunger in himself to be more serious,
> And gravitating with it to this ground,
> Which, he once heard, was proper to grow
>   wise in,
> If only that so many dead lie round.

Larkin and I continued to correspond, my letters long and full of questions, his replies brief. Instead of pictures of Depeche Mode or Madness or skinny Paul Weller, I pinned the poet's letters to a board in my bedroom.

When Larkin died, I got a ticket to his memo-
rial service and sat by myself in the back row.
Years later, I was briefly in Hull for an inter-
view with John Prescott, the former British
deputy prime minister noted for his butchery
of the English language. I stole a few hours
to walk around Larkin's home, with a copy
of his poems bought in the discount pile of a
bookshop for a couple of pounds. But this is
a story about my mother, who cleared out my
bedroom when I got married and threw out
my correspondence with Larkin and many
other things beside. For years she assured me
my letters were in the attic. Finally on one trip
home, I demanded to see the attic with my
archive intact. The attic was bare, no bundles
of letters or any other hoarded goods. She had
decided without asking that I too should be

loyal to the present. I have so much to be grate-ful for with my mother, but honestly, I never forgave her.

⸲

At the house, we existed in a sort of limbo, waiting for the coroner to release the body—'Mrs Ferguson, I mean,' the coroner's assis-tant corrected herself. Anthony and I pored over her address book, bringing the news of her death to her friends, only some of whom we knew. We tried to piece together the last forty-eight hours before she went to hospital, including the night she spent on the floor of her kitchen after she fell, the scene I could not bear to think about. All we knew was that she fell in the daylight and woke in the dark, on the floor, unable to move.

Cosmo arrived from Australia, pale from the winter. We flew so much when I was little that I acquired from my mother the formal habits of 1960s travel. She used to dress us up for flights and once overseas have matching outfits made for the return. I did the same when the boys were little, dressing them in matching jackets—just for flying. Cosmo and Lucien asked gingerly if they could play tennis on the neighbour's court as we had done earlier in the summer. Victorian habits of mourning linger in England and according to that etiquette it would not have been alright. But Marjorie loved tennis, and she would have enjoyed the sounds of their game floating back across the garden to her kitchen. The neighbours, the Cecils, had gone to Nairobi, but they'd told us before leaving to help ourselves to the fruit on their trees. I walked over to watch the boys play tennis and reached for a ripe pear. I sat by the court and watched them as if from far away, briefly envying them their freedom.

∾

One early morning, I lifted the corner of the blind in our room. I saw a triangle of blue. *It must be more bearable with sunshine in the churchyard*, I thought. This was the day of the funeral. The inquest was ahead of us, but they had released the body.

We arrived early at the church, the slow passage of the hearse to the crematorium behind us. Inside, the church was empty except for the wardens making neat piles of the orders of service. The photo on the front showed

Marjorie in a portrait taken for her twenty-
first birthday. It was such a beautiful photo
you couldn't help smiling. This was not the
church I had grown up with, but it was famil-
iar, another Norman building holding nine
centuries of life within the three-foot thick-
ness of its walls. I placed the long bouquet of
meadow flowers from the coffin into the deep
recess of one of the windows. The heavy door
of the church swung open behind me. It was
my friend Lucy. She'd come from the improb-
ably named Helions Bumpstead, a village on
the other side of the county, in a Tarago taxi
with just her and an anxious driver who had
lost his way. My brilliant, beautiful friend
who had shocked my mother on my wedding
day, sitting in the garden, ending a story with
the loud phrase, 'Fuck me sideways, vicar.'

My mother had run inside, almost in tears. Now, Lucy was here for Marjorie when I most needed her. I made her sit with me in the family pews and we sang together, in and out of tune, holding hands.

My role that day was to allow others to enjoy their memories of my mother. If I could smile instead of crying, they could relax and treasure her. My Scottish cousin, dressed in full kilt, read, 'I wandered lonely as a cloud', his voice rich, not unlike my father's, rolling his r's through 'trees' and 'breeze' until the daffodils seemed to fill the church. The grandchildren spoke, each in their own way, of her kindness. When it was Cosmo and Lucien's turn, I was nervous as they approached the pulpit in the silence. They looked foreign standing in this English place, not English at all, I realised with a shock. They all remembered the level way their grandmother spoke to them, her absence of hierarchy. She was formal but not superior with anyone. Hapless tradesmen or telemarketers would ask, 'Can I call you Marjorie?' 'No. Mrs Ferguson,' she would reply. Cosmo described how when he stayed with her they would stay up late eating ice cream and discussing world affairs, armchair diplomatists roaming the world, he said. Lucien spoke in a stronger accent, bringing Sydney into the church. When he was a little boy growing up in Australia, he said, he believed Marjorie was the Queen of England. People smiled, relaxing a little more in the hard wooden pews. He ended with a verse from Coleridge, inserting her name into the final lines,

... For thee our gentle-hearted Marjorie, to
  whom
No sound is dissonant which tells of Life.

Uncle John rose to speak and the atmosphere shifted again; the stones released some of their store of cold. His face was full of grief, his lips and eyes red, his voice quiet, straining through his throat, almost a rasp.

'Yea, thou I walk through the valley of the shadow of death ...'

The mourners left the church and walked across the green to the village pub. We ate and drank, the bonds between my present life and this former one strong for a moment. As night fell, the lingerers became a smaller group, the living going on. Tony and I left the pub and walked back to the darkened church.

The light of the tabernacle glowed red. A single lamp hung in the nave, enough light to see that someone had placed the long bouquet of flowers from the coffin onto the altar. To me those meadow flowers were her resting there, illuminated in the ancient stillness. I sat in the front pew and held her with me.

❧

In Australia I should have followed Jewish custom, stayed at home, let people visit me. But we are not wise in these moments, our custom urging us to 'move on', the cruellest expectation. I didn't just go back to work, I went to America to film a story. For days in a dark, cramped hotel room in New York, I slept the wrong hours and had nightmares. I watched the program go to air, lying on the sofa in the house of close colleagues; as it ended, I began not just to cry but to sob. I couldn't stop, but they understood and took away any discomfort. Going home I met a third kind driver, a Nigerian taxi driver this time, who talked to me about Lagos until we reached the house, where Tony was waiting on the pavement.

❧

In December we returned to England for the inquest. Some questioned my decision to go, suggesting my mother wouldn't want it, but she would. She would expect me to look for answers, fight against cant, hypocrisy and bureaucratic indifference. She would want me to try to make them tell the truth, *to go in to bat*. The coroner's office asked Anthony and I if we wanted lawyers, we said no. Like wanting to carry my father's body, drive his hearse, I wanted us to do this ourselves.

It felt different returning this time. I wasn't coming home to her. She didn't live here anymore. Did I still belong? Anthony was still here, our bond stronger than ever, but with him it was horizontal, the vertical link to history was cut. I felt untethered.

One of my most perceptive friends told me that the conversation with our parents continues after their death. I didn't understand at first, but now in England again I began to hear something. Not my mother's voice exactly, but something like that exquisite sound beginning to be audible.

We moved by train through avenues of thin winter trees and the drab backs of houses towards London. I had an image of her in my mind's eye, the twenty-first birthday photo but including her older self and infinitely gentle. Tears sat behind my eyes, making them ache. If only there was a telephone I could ring to hear her voice, the voice talking to me on the way to primary school, or waiting for me after school at the low brick wall near the little wrought-iron gate. Or the voice on long distance calls I made too infrequently from Australia. I remember arriving at a hotel in Broome, where there was a sign on the wardrobe that said, 'Now call your mother'. So I did. 'Where's Broome?' she said, pulling out a map. She loved maps, knowing where places were, knowing where I was.

'We'll shortly be arriving at Clapham Junction.' The announcement brought me back to the train. Seated next to us were two young women, tourists, both with large hoop earrings and thick false eyelashes, tapping on their phones with long nails. They repeated the station announcement in heavy accents and giggled. At their age, Marjorie boarded a train from Mombasa to Nairobi after the long ship journey from England. She never forgot the train trip, the sounds and smells of Africa, her first sight of brightly dressed Masai women. Imagine the adventure for a young woman who had grown up during the war.

At Anthony's house I opened the heavy grey package containing the hospital's final report. I read their observations through the hours of careless treatment leading to my mother's death. There were hundreds of pages, each with her name at the top, my mother's name written by a stranger. The pages described the fall at home, an ambulance with my mother complaining she didn't want to go, an operation for a fractured hip and just before surgery began, they noted that an embolism, a blood clot, had occurred. The anaesthetist paused but decided to go ahead with the surgery. They knew there were no beds in ICU so they sent her to the recovery ward, which was busy and understaffed. No one called the family to say that she had suffered a life-threatening event. Anthony was in Italy and I was in Melbourne, oblivious to her deteriorating condition. I came to the page with her last recorded words, in a nurse's handwriting. It read, 'Patient says she feels clammy and cold.' The words took my breath away. Couldn't they see what was happening? I struggled to read on, my heart heaving. Just after midnight, the cardiac team was called, they noted the patient looked very unwell. It was twelve hours since the operation. She went into cardiac arrest three times, her eyes rolled back in her head and she died. One of the doctors wrote 'rest in peace' at the bottom of his notes. I got up and went to sit next to Tony on the sofa, holding the report on my knees.

'Why did I think I could read this? No one should read this.'

I waited until the next day then started again from the beginning, making notes as I went, using the instincts of my other self, the journalist not the daughter. So much of death is remembered in poetry, but this was now a story told in prose. The language of the report was alternately patronising and mechanical. The hospital had done its investigation, ten pages concluding there was no alternative outcome. There were 'gaps in her care', but nothing would have made a difference. It read like a hastily written essay, where alternatives had not been properly considered. Friends in Australia quickly put me in touch with medical experts there. Battling the time zone, I sought their help to understand better what to ask.

I read the report again. This time I noticed that amongst the almost 500 pages, one critical page was missing. The page where the anaesthetist who noticed the embolism had laid out the reasons for his decisions to proceed. It wasn't obvious because of the page numbering, but the page was not there. The inquest was about to begin and no one had noticed. It was Friday afternoon. We called the coroner, but they had gone home.

We set off back to my mother's house on Sunday night, the sort of dreary evening that in my twenties had made me leave London for Paris. I sat in the back seat, holding up my phone and reading a paper from the *Canadian Journal of Surgery* titled, 'Preventing Embolisms in Surgery'.

I dreaded the return to my mother's empty house, fearful of burglary, not for the loss of things, but fear of desecration. I also feared the effect of absence. Her presence there must be weak now. A house will punish you if you leave it too long. Anthony pushed open the front door. It was cold inside, very cold. We turned on the lights and our breath was illuminated. The red light flashed on the answering machine. There was a pile of letters on the floor, Christmas cards, mostly from overseas. We ran into the kitchen where the AGA would offer some warmth, but the kitchen was cold too. The temperature gauge was below zero; the heating had broken down. Tony wanted to go to a hotel, but the sensible idea was outlandish to me. I couldn't leave. He and Anthony climbed into the attic and read boiler manuals on their phones, barely able to grip them in the cold. You forget how cold England can be. Sarah and I went upstairs and searched for my mother's scarves and hats and looked for blankets. We built a fire in the log-burning stove with coal. I didn't know you could still burn coal. The heat was paltry. Anthony and his family sat on the sofa under a doona, Sarah wore a puffer jacket and a large pink mohair scarf of my mother's. I lay next to the stove wearing two thick jumpers, Tony wore a jumper, a coat and a ski hat. We watched old episodes of *The West Wing*, too cold to move or think.

I slept late, woken by the neighbours who had come over to look at the boiler, climbing the creaky ladder to the attic. Everyone was up except me. Anthony had slept in a hat and had a long crease on his forehead like a surgical scar. My uncle had arrived and was waiting for breakfast in the chilly kitchen. We were burying my mother's ashes before the inquest began, but I was focused on the last call I had to make to a doctor in Australia for more advice. I sat on the edge of the bed gripping a pen with numb fingers, making notes. There was no hot water, so Tony washed my hair over the bath with water heated in a pan.

I wanted to warm up to collect my thoughts, but my brain felt stiff.

We walked up the gravel path of the churchyard for the second time. The leaves had gone, revealing the red Tudor brick of the church tower. Cardinal Wolsey, the Lord of the Manor, had added the tower in 1530, using bricks from Hampton Court. Whimsically, the top of the tower was built to resemble the cardinal's hat. My mind slipped briefly to *Wolf Hall* and back again as the vicar rolled up his surplice sleeve to check his watch. Behind us a taxi pulled up at the church gate. My faithful nephew had battled broken ATMs and train cancellations to make it on time. There was a man standing off to the side in a morning suit. The under-taker. I hadn't figured on his presence, but of course he had come to supervise the digging of the hole. The vicar knew we were cold and offered tea. We crowded around the radiators in the back room. Anthony's phone rang, he'd had to leave it on for the coroner to call. He and I stood in the church porch with the coroner's assistant on loudspeaker. They had got our message about the missing page and were scrambling a response; did we want to postpone? It was a near impossible question. Part of me wanted to postpone, take more time, do more research, but I knew that everyone else wanted the inquest to be over. We agreed to go ahead if the coroner would read the missing page before we began.

It was a clear beautiful morning with a low sun falling across the frosty graveyard. As we stood around the freshly dug plot,

I could hear the distant drone of cars on the A12 taking traffic and cargo towards the East Anglian ports. Anthony and I hadn't relinquished our roles, we insisted on lowering the small casket. We didn't anticipate the weight or the depth of the hole and almost dropped it. The vicar read his prayers in a clear voice that cut through the cold air, but his order of service had a mistake. In place of Marjorie's name was the name of the last deceased he had buried. He saw it just in time, paused and inserted the correct name. As time elapses, the careful ceremony around death relaxes, mistakes creep in, and while your heart is still raw, the world moves on as it must.

We just made it to the coroner's court in time. There were only a few days before Christmas and the roads were clogged and the car parks full. The staff brought us into the court, and there were chairs for Anthony and me in the front row along from the hospital lawyers. Tony and Sarah sat behind with notepads, like our solicitors. Then Uncle John and my niece and nephew. I couldn't imagine how strange a set of memories this would make for the children. They were grown up and smart, but they had arrived in hospital to find their grandmother already dead, not in the careful atmosphere of intensive care, but in an ordinary bed in a recovery ward where she never should have been. Now they had come to the inquest, to see it through to the end.

I looked around the room. It was functional with an empty row of seats for a jury sometimes called for inquests, the coroner's assistant was seated in the corner and next to her was a chair for the witnesses. The hospital investigators whom we had met months earlier came in clutching bundles of papers. They smiled kindly but quickly, as if they didn't want their lawyers to see. The principal lawyer was seated at the other end of our row, with a paralegal by his side whom I mistook for one of the junior doctors. I realised suddenly I was still wearing one of my mother's jumpers, as a second layer against the morning's cold, a gardening jumper with a big hole at the elbow. I must have looked the picture of a dishevelled, grieving relative. I felt the flicker of an advantage. It was not bad if they thought I was going to be a pushover.

The coroner came in and took her seat, bringing gravity into the bare room. She made a speech about the purpose of an inquest, explaining the rules, that she would only consider evidence that went directly to the cause of death.

I found my voice. 'Can I speak?' I asked, then declared the inadequacy of the process, when the hospital had provided a report days before the hearing with the key page missing and one of the key witnesses not called. The coroner asked again if we wanted to postpone. I felt the enormity of the task pressing in. Tony urged me to carry on, we agreed to do so, but I meant to use the mistakes to our advantage. My reporter self was taking over.

In her opening speech, the coroner indicated she had accepted the hospital's conclusion, that despite the mistakes, there was nothing the doctors could have done that would have changed the outcome. I understood how hard the task was going to be to get anything more than the hospital's blameless version recorded as the cause of death. The only opening she offered was if the lack of care actually caused the death. Tony leaned forward and passed me a sheet of paper—his notes were identical to mine.

The first witness was sworn in. A pathologist who began talking about my mother's post-mortem. It couldn't be real. My brain was going haywire again. I made myself slow down and listen.

Witnesses came and went, some more considerate than others. I asked the young surgeon what had happened when the anaesthetist had decided to proceed with the operation, after the blood clot had occurred. She said it was silent in the theatre, the only thing she remembered was the clock ticking. Eventually, the hospital's senior investigator took the stand. Everything depended on her evidence, for us and for them. She was a kind-looking woman, rather scruffy with an uncertain expression. She had clearly prepared to deliver the one apology they could make without any risk: she was sorry they hadn't called us immediately after the operation. It was a dreadful omission because it meant my mother was alone in the hours leading up to her death. Her regret was sincere, but it wasn't what we had come for.

As the coroner questioned her, I felt them working together towards a conclusion: regrettable but unavoidable. I remembered the phrase of the Australian experts, that they didn't give her the best chance. The doctor argued emphatically that there was no alternative but in a kindly way, as if the truth was too hard for me to hear. The coroner nodded in agreement. I looked at my list of questions and saw they would not give me a path to a different ending.

Then a small opening came. I asked a question about what was done to protect my mother against the possibility of an embolism. Their own notes showed they had ticked a box for preventative measures but no action was taken. The coroner was interested—a ticked box for something that wasn't done? I pushed further, using the information I had learned from the paper I'd read on my iPhone in the car. Weren't there other methods that could be used to protect a patient against a clot? The coroner tried to cut me off, thought I had misunderstood, but the doctor paused, then answered honestly: she conceded there were things they could have done. The hospital lawyer tried to stifle the answer. The coroner seemed surprised by the detail. She asked if I had sought legal advice. No, I answered and looked down. I was just the daughter in the un-darned jumper, but the point settled in the room.

The doctors returned to their argument that despite those possibilities, nothing would have changed the outcome. The coroner summed up the evidence, resuming her confidence in the hospital's position that the death was unavoidable.

Then it was the turn of the hospital lawyer. A confident young man, he made the case he had come to make. He said that according to the evidence, the embolism had occurred before my mother even arrived at the hospital, so the hospital was not to blame. Anthony whispered to me that the pathologist didn't say that. I nodded, pulling out my notes. The lawyer continued, exonerating the hospital, shutting down the avenue for further legal action. He argued that based on the evidence, the coroner should deliver a verdict of 'natural causes'.

I wanted to jump across the table. He had gone too far. After everything we had heard, he wanted to reduce my mother to a single phrase, natural causes. He had claimed the hospital played no role at all, that her death was decided the moment she fell in the kitchen. Without any evidence, he had determined the night she spent on the floor, about which we knew so little, as the moment when her death became inevitable. We will never know, but it's more likely that a series of errors had to line up in an overcrowded hospital with an overworked staff to make her death a certainty. I spoke with all the force I could muster, slowly and deliberately.

'On the evidence,' I said, using their language, 'of the inquest's first witness, the pathologist, no one could say when the embolism occurred. It could have occurred on the operating table when it was observed.' Further to that, the hospital had conceded there were preventative measures that could have been applied and I listed them again for emphasis. I wasn't making the case that any one of those measures would have made a difference, but they *could* have. 'A natural-causes verdict is clearly not supported by the evidence.'

I stopped. The coroner looked at me. She said that she had intended to deliver a short-sentence verdict, was on the verge of doing so, but now she had changed her mind. She would retire and consider a full-narrative verdict. As she spoke I wrote on my notes to Anthony, 'That's a BIG win for us.' He whispered, 'What just happened?'

And then it was the end. The high windows of the courtroom showed blackness outside. We resumed our seats. The coroner said how good it was to see so many of the family there, that it was often not the case. She congratulated us on our advocacy. Then she read an account of the death, dismissing natural causes, allowing the possibility that the failure to apply preventative measures against a life-threatening blood clot may have contributed to her death. It was a small victory, but it was a victory.

She asked us to stand. In that moment it was no longer a debate or a contest for truth. It was about my mother, who was dead. She spoke her name. I struggled to hold myself upright, so I stood straighter, rigid and formal, the only way I knew. Then we had to leave. It was late, the staff wanted to pack up and go home. There was nothing more to say. Uncle John's only comment was that there were a lot of words. I suppose he was right. The lawyer shook my hand, the court usher came to do the same. He said he hadn't seen an inquest like it before. But it didn't change the thing I wanted to change. I wanted my mother to be alive, to have another conversation with her, show her things, tell her about the children. When you leave a coroner's court, as they switch off the lights behind you, as you push through the glass doors into the dark, none of those things are part of your life anymore.

⁂

Before I left her house to return to Australia, I sat by myself in the sitting room for the last time, searching for something in the stillness. Then I stood up and kissed each of the walls, an African custom. Back home her flower-bed had flourished. A dahlia I didn't know we had planted bloomed suddenly. The local gardener who had helped me make the bed, had tended the flowers in the summer heat. There was a second flowering of the white hollyhocks, which filled me with delight.

I can hear her voice a little more now. I dreamed she helped me unpack her sideboard with its plates and bowls from Nigeria, sitting next to me, full of kind advice that I couldn't remember in the morning, but I had heard her clearly. Another wise friend told me we love our mothers more as the years pass after they have died. I think she's right.

I realise now how like her I am. I look like her, I sound like her. I am like her. Our lives have been lived differently, but all the good things she knew, she passed on quietly when I wasn't looking, when I was so convinced I was independent and so utterly different. All along I was hearing what she said and taking it in. I don't apologise for being sad anymore, but I do tell everyone to call their mother.

I'm sure some of my facts are wrong and I know if Anthony were to tell the story of our mother it would come out differently, but we love her together. The Queen of England. Our gentle-hearted Marjorie.

Read
'On'

Little Books,
Big Ideas

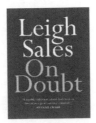

Leigh
Sales
On
Doubt

'A superbly stylish and valuable
little book on this century's great
vanishing commodity.'
Annabel Crabb

Acclaimed journalist Leigh Sales has her doubts, and
thinks you should, too. Her classic personal essay
carries a message about the value of truth, scrutiny and
accountability—a much-needed, pocket-sized antidote
to fake news.

Donald Trump, the post-truth world and the instability
of Australian politics are all examined in this fresh take
on her prescient essay on the media and political trends
that define our times.

Blanche
d'Alpuget
On
Lust &
Longing

'A delicate confession of the implications of lust and
longing on a girl's sexual awakening …'
Marta Dusseldorp

On Lust and *On Longing* together for the first time.

When *On Lust* was first published it caused a media
sensation: Blanche d'Alpuget wrote of a pillar of society
who had molested children and of events that ended in
mystery. Now she reveals all. *On Longing* caused a similar
sensation, for different reasons. D'Alpuget dared to write
that she loved and had inspired love in a man already
adored by the public.

Here are the raw and timeless themes of the power and
powerlessness inherent to lust, love, loss and death.

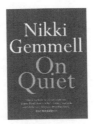

'This is the book we all need right now. Gemmell nails how to achieve serenity and calm amid all the crazy busyness of modern living.'
Lisa Wilkinson

International bestselling author Nikki Gemmell writes on the power of quiet in today's shouty world.

Quiet comes as a shock in these troubled times.

Quietism means 'devotional contemplation and abandonment of the will ... a calm acceptance of things as they are'. Gemmell makes the case for why quiet is steadily gaining ground in this noisy age: Why we need it now more than ever. How to glean quiet, hold on to it, and work within it.

Katharine
Murphy
On
Disruption

The internet has shaken the foundations of life: public and
private lives are wrought by the 24-hour, seven-day-a-week
news cycle that means no one is ever off duty.

On Disruption is a report from the coalface of that change:
what has happened, will it keep happening,
and is there any way out of the chaos?

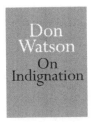

Don
Watson
On
Indignation

Don Watson takes us on a journey of indignation and how
it has been expressed in his forebears. His ire towards US
politicians has a new moving target: Donald Trump.

The US President's primary pitch had less to do with
giving people money or security than it was about
vengeance. Trump exploited the anger we feel when
we are slighted or taken for granted, turning the politics
of a sophisticated democracy into something more like a
blood feud. He promised to restore their dignity, slay their
enemies, re-make the world according to old rites and
customs. He stirred their indignation into tribal rage and
rode it into the White House.

It was a scam, of course, but wherever there is indignation,
lies and stupidity abound.

On Sleep is the story of our love–hate relationship
with slumber.

Part-time insomniac Fleur Anderson ponders the big
questions: Why can't I sleep? Do politicians and other
high-fliers ever admit they too are exhausted? Do they get
enough sleep to make sensible decisions? Where is society
heading, and why did I have that glass of cab sav?